ENGAGING
PARENTS & CARERS
WITH SCHOOL

ENGAGING PARENTS & CARERS WITH SCHOOL

{ Emma Kell
Clemmie Stewart }

SAGE Publications Ltd
1 Oliver's Yard
55 City Road
London EC1Y 1SP

Corwin
A SAGE company
2455 Teller Road
Thousand Oaks, California 91320
(800)233-9936
www.corwin.com

SAGE Publications India Pvt Ltd
B 1/I 1 Mohan Cooperative Industrial Area
Mathura Road
New Delhi 110 044

SAGE Publications Asia-Pacific Pte Ltd
3 Church Street
#10-04 Samsung Hub
Singapore 049483

© Emma Kell and Clemmie Stewart 2023

Apart from any fair dealing for the purposes of research, private study, or criticism or review, as permitted under the Copyright, Designs and Patents Act, 1988, this publication may not be reproduced, stored or transmitted in any form, or by any means, without the prior permission in writing of the publisher, or in the case of reprographic reproduction, in accordance with the terms of licences issued by the Copyright Licensing Agency. Enquiries concerning reproduction outside those terms should be sent to the publisher.

Editor: Delayna Spencer
Editorial assistant: Bali Birch-Lee
Production editor: Martin Fox
Copyeditor: Sarah Bury
Proofreader: Thea Watson
Indexer: Elske Janssen
Marketing manager: Dilhara Attygalle
Cover design: Wendy Scott
Typeset by: C&M Digitals (P) Ltd, Chennai, India
Printed in the UK

**Library of Congress Control Number:
2022944585**

**British Library Cataloguing in Publication
data**

A catalogue record for this book is available
from the British Library

ISBN 978-1-5297-9632-2 (pbk)

At SAGE we take sustainability seriously. Most of our products are printed in the UK using responsibly sourced papers and boards. When we print overseas we ensure sustainable papers are used as measured by the PREPS grading system. We undertake an annual audit to monitor our sustainability.

TABLE OF CONTENTS

{ ABOUT THIS BOOK }

A Little Guide for Teachers: Engaging Parents and Carers with Schools builds on author experience, and findings from the spotlight thrown on home–school relationships during Covid-19, to provide teachers with effective strategies to enhance these relationships and instill confidence in teachers working with parents.

The Little Guide for Teachers series is little in size but BIG on all the support and inspiration you need to navigate your day-to-day life as a teacher.

- Authored by experts in the field
- Easy to dip in-and-out of
- Interactive activities encourage you to write into the book and make it your own
- Read in an afternoon or take as long as you like with it!

Find out more at
www.sagepub.co.uk/littleguides

{ ABOUT THE SERIES }

A LITTLE GUIDE FOR TEACHERS series is little in size but big on all the support and inspiration you need to navigate your day-to-day life as a teacher.

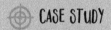 CASE STUDY

 EXERCISES

HINTS & TIPS

REFLECTION

IDEAS FOR THE CLASSROOM

NOTE IT DOWN

NOTE IT DOWN!

WITH THAT IN MIND, JOT DOWN WHAT YOU WISH YOUR PARENTS KNEW BEFORE THEIR CHILDREN GOT TO YOUR CLASS OR KEY STAGE.

- WHAT I WISH THEY KNEW
- WHAT I WISH THEIR CHILDREN COULD DO
- HOW PARENTS MIGHT BE ABLE TO SUPPORT THAT
- HOW I MIGHT COMMUNICATE THAT

TAKE EVERY 'WISH, I WISH THEY COULD JUST _____ FOR THEMSELVES' AND SHARE THAT BEFORE THE CHILD GETS TO YOU!

ABOUT THE AUTHORS

Dr Emma Kell has over two decades' experience as a teacher and leader in UK secondary schools and is a qualified Performance Coach. Emma currently teaches in Alternative Provision, and is mum to two girls and several animals. She speaks and facilitates regularly on teacher wellbeing, recruitment and retention. She writes for a variety of publications including TES and BBC Teach. Emma has completed a doctorate on teacher well-being and parenting at Middlesex University. Emma is author of *How To Survive in Teaching* (Bloomsbury, 2018) and co-author of *A Little Guide For Teachers: Wellbeing and Self-Care* (SAGE, 2020).

Clemmie Stewart is a Director of Learning and Teaching for a schools group, working across schools in the UK and internationally. Previously she has held leadership roles cross sector, including most recently being a Head across two schools in London. She is a governor of two schools in a MAT and has delivered a TEDx talk on the impact of parenting on resilience in children. When not talking, writing about or working in education, you can find her running, in the gym or with her puppy.

ACKNOWLEDGEMENTS

With thanks to David Fisher, Headteacher; Raj Unsworth, Governor; and Dominic Norrish, COO.

And all of our survey participants, for your generosity, honesty and wisdom when we consulted you for this book.

This book is dedicated to our parents, for their neverending support and encouragement.

CHAPTER 1
WHY DOES PARENTAL ENGAGEMENT MATTER?

This chapter explores the ideas that:

- Parents, carers and teachers are united in wanting the best for children: focusing on this is key
- Challenges to effective home–school engagement include fear and mistrust on both sides, a lack of effective training in some schools and time-pressures
- Opportunities for effective home–school engagement include a sense of community, greater lines of communication and an appreciation of school staff.

KEY PRINCIPLES – WHAT THIS BOOK IS AND WHAT IT ISN'T...

We're not in the business of telling people how to teach – and we're certainly not out to tell parents and carers how to parent. This isn't a teaching or parenting manual. We appreciate that with this little guide, we've taken on a huge, tricky and often highly emotive subject. We appreciate that 'parenting' comes in a myriad of different forms and we use the term 'parent' to refer to parents and carers in all their forms. We also appreciate the need to embrace a wide range of voices and perspectives and this book will act to signpost areas where more research would be welcomed. We avoid some of the sweeping generalisations sometimes heard in staffrooms and playgrounds. Instead of 'hard-to-reach' parents, we consider 'hard-to-reach' schools; instead of 'difficult' parents or 'unapproachable' staff, we look at the factors which might contribute to these challenges and offer research-based and practical approaches which have worked in schools.

This guide is for teachers and school staff in all roles, working in both the state and independent sectors. While research has taken place predominantly in the UK, as this is where both authors are based, findings may also be useful internationally.

THE RESEARCH

A significant amount of the material in our book is based on our own experience in schools, totalling over 30 years and based on a range of primary, secondary, state, alternative, special needs and mainstream settings and in governance roles. We also come into contact regularly with fellow staff in schools and their experiences find their way into our findings, though they are completely anonymised. In order to capture key contemporary themes and ensure our data is robust, we undertook two surveys – one for parents and carers and one for staff working in schools. The surveys included both qualitative and quantitative responses and asked for responses about the:

- Impact of Covid-19 on home–school relationships

- Quality of relationships between parents and schools

- Evolving nature of engagement between parents and schools as children get older

- Biggest challenges in terms of home–school engagement for parents and teachers respectively

- Most positive elements of home–school engagement for parents and teachers respectively.

228 participants responded to the parent-carer survey and 313 school staff to the one aimed at teachers, school leaders, pastoral leaders and teaching assistants.

THE HOME–SCHOOL RELATIONSHIP MATTERS

When asked how important parental engagement with schools is, the consensus is unanimous. 'It's crucial', said one governor. 'It's everything!' In our survey, 98% of parents and carers and 97% of school staff agreed or strongly agreed that a strong relationship between home and school is important.

The research supports this view. Harris and Goodall (2007: 7) summarise the importance of effective parental engagement as follows:

> The research evidence is consistent, in demonstrating that families have a major influence on their children's achievement in school and through life. When schools, families and community work together to support learning, children tend to do better in school, stay in school longer and like school more.

Children are like sponges. Learning takes place constantly and the messages they receive at home mean even more than those they receive at school. Kallivayalil and Thomas (2019) remind us that the parent is the child's first and ongoing teacher and that students with strong support from home 'have achieved better grades at school and grown up with a higher self-esteem'.

ECOLOGICAL SYSTEMS THEORY

Bronfenbrenner's ecological systems theory provides a powerful model that highlights the crucial and intertwined factors that influence children, families and schools (Figure 1.1).

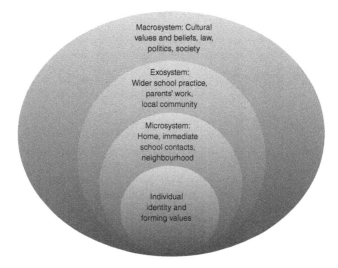

Figure 1.1   Ecological systems: Families and schools (our interpretation of a model based on Bronfenbrenner's ecological theory (1979))

 REFLECTION

Consider your school community, class or an individual student. Adapt the ecological model to consider the influences on their learning and development.

How are the following factors affecting their evolving identity and values?

Microsystem: home, teachers, support staff, office staff, canteen staff (immediate school contacts)

Exosystem: school policies and procedures, school values and practices, parental work (or lack thereof), community contacts

Macrosystem: government policy, cost of living, cultural norms

What steps can you take in your role to positively influence this development? Where can you have greatest impact?

WHAT UNITES PARENTS AND SCHOOLS?

The differences that separate human beings are nothing compared to the similarities that bond us together.
Sophie Grégoire Trudeau (Phillips, 2016)

The difference between schools and many other businesses is that it's all about humans – living organisms, working with other living organisms. This can feel complex and daunting at times, but the home–school relationship is, at its root, very simple:

Parents and teachers want the best for children.

In the words of one parent, we want our children to be happy, healthy and kind. Success, confidence, resilience, drive and focus all come into it too, but ultimately what unites us as adults devoted to young people is greater than what divides us.

In the words of another parent:

> Cut the crap. How can we work together to give my children the best experience? (Parent survey participant)

Attention management for busy teachers is key. We could tie ourselves in knots dwelling on misunderstandings and falling into defensiveness, but it doesn't help anything. Consider what parents want for their children. Research conducted by Robbins and Dempster (2021) reveals that starting a conversation with test results is unlikely to create a bond. Children's happiness is the priority.

 EXERCISE

Do parents know how much they matter?

We've established that parents really, really matter to the successful learning and development of children. Do they know how much they matter in your organisation or classroom? What evidence do you have to demonstrate this? Using the key criteria from Harris and Goodall (2007), take time with other members of staff to consider to what extent:

1   Parents are supporting learning at home.

2   The school offers bespoke support to parents from socio-economic and ethnic groups less likely to engage with school.

3   There is mutual trust and respect between parents and teachers.

4   Parents and schools are jointly committed to improving learning outcomes.

5   Parents and schools work effectively together on positive behaviour.

6   The school prioritises parental engagement.

7   Staff feel confident and competent when engaging with parents.

As you work through the rest of this book, consider what strategies you might adopt to ensure effective working relationships with parents.

Based on Harris and Goodall (2007)

SOCIAL AND HISTORICAL FACTORS INFLUENCING PARENTAL ENGAGEMENT

COVID-19

The impact of the Covid-19 pandemic on mental health is an acute and ongoing concern. Factors likely to influence poor mental health include:

- Social isolation (including those shielding)
- Job loss and financial loss
- Housing insecurity and quality
- Reduced access to mental health services.

This is likely to affect both our students and their parents.

As we write this book, the coronavirus pandemic continues to influence all aspects of human existence. The 'gaps' in society which existed before the outbreak have turned into huge crevasses. As highlighted by the *Covid-19 Social Study* (UCL, 2020), people who were vulnerable before the pandemic are likely to be even more vulnerable now. This ongoing study highlights the following (as of November 2021):

- Widening socio-economic inequalities: 'Those who were struggling financially before the pandemic have consistently been more than twice as likely to say they are worse off than those who were living comfortably (assessed in June and November 2020 and October 2021).' (Report – week 81–84)

- Those from low-income households (less than 30k pa) reported higher levels of depression, anxiety and loneliness. (Report – week 81–84)

- Worries about accessing sufficient food affect around one in eight: 'These concerns are higher in people with a mental or physical health diagnosis and people with lower household incomes.' (Report – week 77–80)

- Nearly half of adults (44%) reported having experienced some kind of discrimination (e.g., due to gender, age, race/ethnicity, or some other characteristic) since the start of the pandemic. (Report – week 73–76)

THE IMPACT OF THE PANDEMIC ON MENTAL HEALTH

The mental health crisis has had a profound effect on young people. The Coalition for Youth Mental Health in Schools (2021) reported the following startling findings. The findings were based on seven focus groups of teachers, parents and young people. Compared to before the pandemic:

- **62%** of young people reported feeling **anxious or worried** more frequently

- **46%** reported feeling a **continuous low mood or sadness** more frequently

- **42%** reported **not getting any enjoyment out of life** more frequently

- **38%** reported feeling **hopeless or tearful** more frequently

- **18%** reported having **suicidal thoughts** more frequently.

Parents, too, have suffered as a result of the pandemic, with sharp rises in depression and anxiety. Unsurprisingly, the groups most affected are those who are socially isolated, have suffered from financial losses and are living in poor or insecure housing.

The effects of such a mental health crisis are likely to be long-lasting and significant, which means the 'business as usual' messages from Ofsted (Office for Standards in Education, Children's Services and Skills) and the government and the focus on academic standards and attendance seem starkly at odds with an urgent need to nurture children and families.

HOME–SCHOOL RELATIONSHIPS: CHALLENGES

FEAR AND MISTRUST

When Emma first started teaching, it was a good three years before she could pick up the phone to a parent without a sense of sick fear at the pit of her stomach. Many new teachers feel the same. As a parent, Emma positively quaked when pre-school announced they were doing a 'home visit' and spent a whole day cleaning the house.

What's this about? At its heart, on both sides, there is a fear of judgement. Is the teacher basically rubbish at their job? Is there a suggestion the parent has failed in their duty of care to their child?

Acknowledging the causes of this fear and mistrust in order to overcome them is absolutely key.

A LACK OF TRAINING

Startlingly, our research has revealed a distinct lack of quality training for teachers when working with parents. In our survey, a striking 73% of teachers disagreed or strongly disagreed with the statement 'My initial training for my role prepared me effectively to work with parents', and 83% with the statement 'I receive regular and meaningful professional development on working with parents'. Perhaps more worryingly, this issue is not lost on parents, with only 38% agreeing or strongly agreeing with the statement

'It is clear that teachers at our school/institution have been well trained to work effectively with parents'.

TIME!

Teachers are notorious for being perceived as 'busy'. The plethora of initiatives and priorities in schools makes this understandable, but frankly, not acceptable as a reason for not engaging effectively with parents.

When it comes to parents, schools are sometimes guilty of forgetting that they have lives and jobs too. Consideration of parents' own priorities when scheduling parental consultation events, assemblies and other school events is key.

HOME–SCHOOL RELATIONSHIPS: OPPORTUNITIES

A SENSE OF COMMUNITY

With the pandemic has come a heightened sense of community. When the pandemic hit, many schools set to work ensuring their children's most basic needs were met before worrying too much about learning and progress. Food parcels, art packages, and reading books were delivered to homes all over the country and the precious impact of this on relationships should not be underestimated. There was a sense of schools being the centre, the hub of the community. New communalities were discovered – parents found that teachers, too, were struggling with vulnerable relatives, teaching their own children at home and worrying about catching the virus. These lessons learned have been profound and must be cherished and built on.

GREATER LINES OF COMMUNICATION

Communication pathways between parents and schools have been strengthened by the pandemic. Schools which took the time to phone the homes of students on a regular basis to check on their progress and wellbeing have gained an increased sense of trust from parents. Knowing that somebody cares enough to take the time to pick up the phone goes a long way. While this has come with its challenges (see Chapter 5), improved levels of IT literacy mean that the potential for sharing student progress, resolving issues promptly and maintaining positive relationships is huge.

AN APPRECIATION OF TEACHERS

The flurry of memes on social media depicting parents tearing their hair out as they tried to educate their own children, while maintaining their own responsibilities, revealed in many cases a new-found respect of teachers. 'You have 30 of them? I can't even handle one!' Many parents took time to get their heads around the curriculum (the memory of puzzling out the inner angles of irregular polygons makes my head hurt to this day!). While the media portrayals of teachers sometimes caused frustration, knowing our parents appreciate us goes a long way and provides a valuable new base to build on.

We can only hope this trend continues...

NOTE IT DOWN!

HAVING READ THIS CHAPTER, NOW IDENTIFY AND NOTE DOWN:

YOUR BIGGEST PROFESSIONAL CHALLENGE WHEN ENGAGING WITH PARENTS

YOUR BIGGEST OPPORTUNITIES OR SOURCES OF OPTIMISM WHEN ENGAGING WITH PARENTS

CHAPTER 2
INDIVIDUAL NEEDS

This chapter explores the ideas that:

- We are a long way from achieving true equity in schools: can children and their parents see themselves in your school?
- Inclusive spaces and formative conversations really matter
- Clear lines of communication are key and a focus on the positive makes a huge difference.

> *The things that make me different are the things that make me.*
> Piglet (Arends, 2003)

In starting this chapter, we searched high and low for quotations that could best summarise the wonderful and unique nature of each and every child we encounter. Many scholarly articles later, and the great philosopher Piglet seems to capture it best. Each young person who enters our classroom will bring with them a multitude of experiences, characteristics, strengths, passions and quirks.

EQUITY AND DIVERSITY

> *You can't be what you can't see.*
> Marian Wright Edelman, Founder and President of the Children's
> Defense Fund (Siebel Newsom, 2011)

Personal development of young people now forms a core component of how the quality of schools' provision is evaluated (Ofsted, 2021). As we have established, the personal development of children is closely entwined with the identities of their parents and families. The onus is on schools to ensure that diversity is not just 'tolerated' but actively celebrated. In the words of Ofsted (2021), schools need to:

- Advance equality of opportunity between persons who share a relevant protected characteristic and persons who do not share it

- Foster good relations between persons who share a relevant protected characteristic and persons who do not share it.

Blessedly, the days of assuming all children come from tight nuclear families are behind us, but there is still significant work to do to ensure that our children and families show respect for a diverse range of people, particularly in relation to the protected characteristics:

- Age
- Disability
- Gender reassignment
- Marriage and civil partnership
- Pregnancy and maternity
- Race
- Religion or belief
- Sex
- Sexual orientation.

Schools are microcosms of society. While a deep exploration of the issue falls beyond the scope of this book (see Bennie Kara's *A Little Guide for Teachers: Diversity in Schools* (2020) for a much more in-depth insight), it is essential that we highlight that cultures of true equity are a long way off for most schools. A research study by UCL in 2020 revealed that 46% of schools have no Black, Asian and Minority Ethnic (BAME) teachers (UCL, 2020), just 36% of secondary school Headteachers (compared to 62% of the workforce) are female, while the vast majority of teaching assistants are women, according to recent data from Wales (Morgan, 2019). Only 5% of school governors in 2021 were from ethnic minorities. Can you honestly say that your children and families can 'see themselves' within the power structures of your schools?

Meanwhile, 'awareness' days, weeks and months risk coming across as patronising and tokenistic. True equity is part of the fabric of every school. Consider families who don't directly identify with one specific group – many will identify with more than one group. Other families still might not directly identify with (or 'tick the box' for) a specific group – a school in Buckinghamshire is aware that families from Gypsy, Roma or Traveller communities will often not identify as such due to stigma with the local community.

With many parents feeling isolated, frustrated and polarised, what are your parents seeing, hearing and experiencing when they interact with your school?

 REFLECTION

Consider some of the following:

> **Can families see themselves in your school? Consider staffing, displays, dress codes for staff, food and drink...**

> **How does your school deal with discrimination in the form of micro-aggressions?**

> **Is there a chance that some families may face unconscious bias or unjustified presumptions when they come into school?**

> **How are religious festivals and practices honoured and celebrated in your school?**

> **Do you have interpreters and translators on hand to help parents who don't speak English access the school?**

We spend more time discussing how feeling included can benefit relationships between parents and schools in Chapter 3.

SPECIAL EDUCATIONAL NEEDS AND DISABILITIES

For parents of children who struggle at school, advocating for their child's needs can feel like a constant battle. While factors like lack of funding fall outside schools' control, there is much we can do at school to reassure these families that we are on the same side and that their child's needs really matter.

In this section, we explore how to work with the parents of children with individual needs: for some, this will be considered special educational needs and disabilities (SEND), but for many others, it is an area that is individual to that child, who may need some additional support and care, with or without a diagnosis. By addressing individual needs, and supporting parents with this, we can hopefully enable more children to have a sense of pride and success from the things that make them who they are.

 REFLECTION

Reflect on the most formative conversation you have had with a parent of a child with SEND or other individual needs.

- **What made it so successful?**

- **What were the ingredients?**

- **What part did you play in that conversation?**

Now think of one that felt tricky or left you feeling that it could have gone better.

- **What was the issue?**

- **When you replayed it – as we all do – what do you wish you could have done differently?**

(Continued)

Jot down your ingredients for a formative conversation below. We will revisit it at the end of the chapter.

A HEADTEACHER EXAMPLE

When I did this activity myself, I thought back to the many parents with whom I have worked to best support their child. When successful, some of the factors that came to mind are:

- I was in receiver mode rather than deliverer: 'Tell me about your child and I will listen'.

- I recognised the parents as an expert in the field – they have lived with and loved every part of that child and I only have them for a small window.

- I suspended my desire to jump in with solutions but listened actively.

- I worked out what I needed to learn more about and committed to doing that before the next conversation.

- We made an informal agreement that we were in partnership and left the conversation feeling like a powerful team.

CODE OF PRACTICE

When writing this chapter, we revisited the SEND Code of Practice (Department for Education and Department of Social Care, 2014) and were once again blown away by the sheer size of the document. On the one hand, this is positive as it shows the importance and emphasis placed on what it is saying. However, as a parent (and indeed as an educator) it is a meaty tome that needs a great deal of unpicking and understanding. Add in the need-specific information about your child, how the school interprets that and any additional health needs and you have parents needing an equivalent to a PhD just to navigate the system. The complexity of this has once again been raised in the 2022 Green Paper (Department for Education, 2022).

The document makes very clear the need for children and parents to be involved in discussions and decision making, which evidences the need for a strong and formative relationship between home and school. The paper itself acknowledges the challenge in stating:

> At times, parents, teachers and others may have differing expectations of how a child's needs are best met. Sometimes these discussions can be challenging but it is in the child's best interests for a positive dialogue between parents, teachers and others to be maintained, to work through points of difference and establish what action is to be taken. (Department for Education and Department of Social Care, 2014)

In recognising and acknowledging this challenge, it also creates an early opportunity to plan and prepare for how to build that relationship, and to ensure that all sides can work cohesively to achieve the very best for each child.

PARENTS OF CHILDREN WITH INDIVIDUAL NEEDS

We find ourselves at risk of making sweeping generalisations in such a short chapter, so please let us start with a health warning that we are gathering a range of views and experiences and combining them. We absolutely recognise that each and every child is unique, as is their home situation and their parents' experience of their learning journey. The additional generalisation 'parents of SEND children' is also unhelpful as it does not recognise the myriad educational needs, disabilities, challenges or barriers faced by our children. However, it does help us to focus on a core group of parents, whom we all want to be supporting and celebrating, so that we can build more effective partnerships. Unsurprisingly, the Covid-19 pandemic has left many parents of children with additional needs feeling raw, unheard and unsupported by many agencies. This can present itself as a significant challenge for staff on the front line and the relationships therein. The gaps continue to widen.

Interestingly, when gathering our research for this book, some of the strongest responses (i.e., strongly agree or strongly disagree) came from parents who identified themselves as having children with SEND. Many parents strongly agreed that their school works effectively with parents of SEND children. However, of all those who responded disagree or strongly disagree, 71% were parents of SEND children. Clearly something has gone wrong for many parents.

THE ROLE OF THE SENDCo

We have an enormous amount of respect for SEND coordinators (SENDCos), many of whom in smaller schools hold extra responsibilities and roles in addition to their extensive work supporting children with diagnosed, and sadly all too often undiagnosed, special educational needs and disabilities. Often, these SENDCos hold almost guru-like status within their setting. How many times have you come up against a barrier with a child, and thought, 'I'll get _____ [insert name of a phenomenal colleague] to come in and have a look. They'll know what to do!' I certainly did this many times with the team of incredible SEND teachers and assistants that I have worked with over the years.

Not only have SENDCos done lengthy and challenging training to be in the role, but they also amass a great deal of skills and knowledge that help to support, nurture and develop each child in their care. These are children who often show a broad range of needs and challenges. They will often lead on the mind-boggling administrative aspect of the role, and will liaise with parents throughout the process.

 # REFLECTION

Think about the lines of communication in your school.

- **When do you seek support for a child whom you think might be showing SEND?**

- **What are the systems for doing that?**

- **At what point does a child become considered as having SEND?**

- **At that point, who is responsible for that child and their learning?**

- **Who is the point of contact for parents?**

Through answering these questions, you may well feel clear and satisfied that this is working in your school. However, you may also identify points where it is less clear, where there are either too many people involved, or not enough. Who is leading on designing the right approach for a child, and who is communicating that with all stakeholders?

Parents also recognise this. One comment in our research was very telling on this point:

> The SENDCo works effectively with parents of SEN students, but less so the class teacher.

Similarly, a member of educational staff who responded to our survey wrote:

> Often communication is done solely through the SENDCo.

Are we, in our haste to show that we are dealing with each pupil in a timely and appropriate manner, being too quick to pass that responsibility to the SENDCo? In doing so, we might be losing the chance to have powerful and meaningful dialogue with parents, and also deskilling ourselves as teachers.

 ## HINTS AND TIPS

It is key at this stage to point out that none of us can be experts in all things. We are huge believers in asking those who know more than we do. Often this will be the SENDCo, but it can also be the teaching assistant who works closely with the child in question, or the midday supervisor who sees them interacting on the playground. Ask for as much information as you can so that you can go into conversations armed with knowledge. Alongside this is the need to do your homework.

- **Have you read every report that has been written about the child in question?**

- **Do you understand what it means?**

- **What did you garner from the teacher who taught them before you?**

- **Have you read through any core communication that has happened between home and school?**

At best, this leads to fertile soil in which you can grow your relationship, showing that you have made the time to really understand this child and their context. And if things get tricky, forewarned is forearmed!

TRICKY CONVERSATIONS

One quote from a surveyed parent really interested us:

> It was as if they were frightened to say the wrong thing or suggest the wrong thing.

They went on to say that the communication was often:

> ...left to the support assistant to do all the communication and although this was great in their part, I would have valued direct communication from the class teacher.

There is so much to unravel here, and it is great to see the support assistant being recognised for playing their part. It did make us wonder why the teacher was not reaching out. It could be the old devil of time – and there never being enough of it. Or was it the parent's perception that there was a fear around saying the wrong thing or causing upset? We know from personal experience that this is a real fear. None of us went into education to upset people or criticise their child; so many of us always seek to celebrate the good bits! However, by skirting around the observations we are making, and not giving parents a clear picture, we are in fact deskilling and disempowering the very team we need to bring out the best in the children we collectively care about. One respondent to our survey wrote:

> When a teacher is truly happy to work in partnership, it can be brilliant as I know my child then gets the support and consistency they need. Openness is key.

HINTS AND TIPS

- Refer to Chapter 4 that covers challenging conversations and use the scaffold to script a conversation you need to have with a parent.

- Work with a trusted colleague to role play the conversation. You could consider asking a third colleague to observe and offer feedback on how you manage.

- For SEND children in your class, have to hand a few bullet points of their core needs and how you are supporting them, as well as progress made over the year.

- Get to know those parents informally and formally: learn their names and how they like to be addressed; know the best way to contact them; make sure they know the people who are working with their child. Short, sharp updates will always be welcome, so involve them in the process.

- Share the good news stories as and when they come.

GOOD NEWS STORIES!

When asked what they enjoy most about the home–school partnership, one parent wrote: 'Feeling like a team focusing on my child.' Who doesn't want to be part of that team?

Similarly, when asked the same question, a member of school staff wrote:

> While parents do not usually have the professional capacity to diagnose a child's needs, they will know the child best and always know when something isn't right. We need to value their voice and involve them in decisions.

This shared desire to work in partnership unites both parties and shows a clear ambition to have open, honest dialogue around the child. Hopefully, the tips above will help both partners to do that.

At the start of the chapter, we asked you to jot down the ingredients for a positive and formative conversation with a parent. What would you now add, and how can that be turned into some useful guidance for your whole team? How might you move that forward to support all colleagues to build powerful relationships with all parents, in particular those of children with SEND?

 **CASE STUDY**

One story shared with us was from a family with a little boy, Ollie, with a range of physical and medical challenges, all of which were captured in his Education and Health Care Plan (EHCP). As he moved from the Early Years Foundation Stage (EYFS) to Key Stage 1, his parents wanted to explore schools where his needs could be best supported and where he could feel very much part of the mainstream environment, despite his physical challenges and differences. The parents' perception was that in several schools they were met with an attitude of 'we will do what we can but there are limitations to what we can offer'. While they recognised that there would of course be challenges that needed to be overcome, they wanted the school to start from a position of positivity and open-mindedness, in the hope that this would transcend into all aspects of their son's education.

Fast forward through a lot of detail and wrangling with the local authority, and Ollie is now flourishing in his setting. He has access to an amazing Learning Support Assistant (LSA) who supports his physical needs, but leaves him to learn and

(Continued)

grow independently in the classroom. He has lots of friends and takes part in all physical aspects of his curriculum, with a focus on the sports that do not pose a risk to him. Every reasonable adjustment is made and his parents have weekly communications with the school to work in partnership to share information, update each other on other specialist agencies and their work, and to check that all is still well. As ever, there is no crystal ball to determine how life will unfold for Ollie, but at this point in time, Team Ollie is working in partnership with a shared ethos, approach and set of hopes and aims to help him thrive.

Stephen Tierney (2020: 21) captures the need to embrace collaboration when supporting every individual:

> When education and learning are viewed from a purely individualistic perspective, this fails to grasp the importance of the 'we'. The role education can play in the formation of relationships, communities and a cohesive society may be lost. But if education lacks a focus on the individual, the importance of 'I' is lost.

As with all things in education, it is a balancing act!

NOTE IT DOWN!

Imagine Ollie was joining your school, or think of a pupil like Ollie for whom you have responsibility.

What might you do to make parents feel that genuine sense of partnership?

What actions might you need to take?

Where might you need to seek support?

CHAPTER 3
RELATIONSHIPS

This chapter explores the ideas that:

- Teachers must be mindful of the power they yield when building relationships
- True inclusion is at the heart of positive home–school relationships and the small things really matter
- The factors which make parents 'hard-to-reach' are complex
- Schools must make themselves 'easy-to-reach' to build positive relationships.

> *They may forget what you said – but they will never forget how you made them feel.*
> Carl W. Buehner (Evans, 1971)

The quality of relationships between parent and school staff is fundamental to a child's happiness and success. Establishing and maintaining positive and enduring home–school relationships requires persistence, time, effort and attention to detail. The obstacles and the pitfalls are numerous, as we've discussed, but ultimately everyone benefits from making this a key school priority.

WIELD YOUR POWER WITH CARE

It's all too easy to forget just how much power we, as professional educators, hold in the eyes of the families we work with. This is rooted in complex systems of social class and in the fact that parents are handing over their most precious of loved-ones every school day in the belief or hope that they will be kept safe and allowed to flourish. Teachers might feel inadequate or stressed when working with parents but, regardless of how little experience you imagine you have, it's essential to remember how much power you hold. Building trust is key to empowering parents and thus building positive relationships. In her thesis on the subject, Taylor (2015) suggests the following:

> Parents trust teachers more when teachers seem involved, when they reach out, when there are frequent communications both formal and informal and both positive and negative.

When building relationships with parents, making use of multiple forms of communication, from a formal parents' evening to asking after the health of the family pet at the school gates, is key. And remember, parents will often expect you to reach out first to break down barriers.

RELATIONSHIPS MATTER: THE SMALL THINGS

While home–school agreements and big mission statements are significant, the small things *really* matter. Whole relationships can be made or broken through the most seemingly insignificant of interactions: the time taken to reassure a parent that the child who howled at drop-off is now settled happily in the reading corner; a misunderstanding over a piece of homework that dominated Sunday evening at home. Parents who feel relationships with school are negative will often cite the apparently smallest of incidents – feeling ignored by a teacher at drop-off, having their name forgotten, a tired teacher inadvertently appearing snappy or irritable...

CRITICAL INCIDENTS

A critical incident is a key moment in time, usually based around an interaction between human beings, which marks a turning point in a relationship, attitudes or mindset.

 REFLECTION

Use the space below to depict the journey you have been on in your relationships with two (sets of) parent(s): one fruitful and positive and the other challenging or difficult. You may wish to use a series of bullet points or a graph, where upward movement indicates a boost to or improvement in the relationships and downward movement indicates a deterioration.

(Continued)

What patterns do you notice? What have you learned from this experience?

Some of the incidents might be obviously significant and include things like:

- A prize giving event

- An exceptional piece of homework

- A significant illness

- An exclusion.

However, we suspect that most incidents will have appeared minor at the time but carried huge significance for the parents, such as:

- Remembering the name of a relative or pet

- Asking them for their advice or expertise in a certain area

- Remembering how they take their tea

- Mispronouncing their name

- Forgetting to call them back when you promised you would

- Being late for a scheduled meeting.

 CASE STUDY

In April 2022, Emma's husband was in Ukraine as the Russian army invaded the country. Her daughters are old enough to be aware of what is happening. The situation is volatile and unpredictable and the emotional strain on the family is huge. Emma emails the school to let them know the situation and within 12 minutes she has a reply from a form tutor. The school quietly intervenes, managing class discussions on the subject with sensitivity and offering the girls 'time out' and a safe space if they need it. This is like a load lifted off the family's shoulders, knowing the girls feel secure and looked after during school hours.

BUILDING RELATIONSHIPS THROUGH INCLUSIVE COMMUNICATION

Many of our parents may have had poor experiences of school, bringing that familiar sense of dread to any potential relationship, together with their own physical and emotional barriers and sets of assumptions. We cannot rewrite history, but we can acknowledge it and seek to make things better and more comfortable. Similarly, parents will have differing work patterns and schedules, impacting on their ability to be present. One easy way to address all of this is taking the time to get to know the parents in our classes, much in the same way as we do our children. This can require creativity. For example, for many parents, a 'cold telephone call' from school might not get a positive response (or any response at all!), whereas a text message might have more chance of a positive reaction. For some parents, a willing and listening ear is a great opportunity to offload their worries about their child, and life in general, while others may be fiercely protective of their privacy. As the relationship grows, they are more likely to disclose to you their feelings around school, their experiences and what impact that might have on their involvement with the school.

Another key consideration is how we address parents, both directly and to the children. Many parents feel very strongly about this, with differing preferences! Mum and Dad can be deemed to be very patronising, and may well be inaccurate. Mr or Ms is polite, but are you sure you have the right surname, or the right gender? Even when writing the title of this book, we debated about the right term to use, taking into account how many different adults may be caring for children. In short, there are bound to be localised school procedures, and you will work out what works for you. One solution would be to ask parents at the start of the year how they wish to be addressed, adding this information at the top of the child's file and parent's evening notes.

 ## IDEAS FOR THE CLASSROOM

To create a truly inclusive space for parents, have you thought about doing the following:

- **Making clear the ways that parents can get hold of you – could you display that information somewhere for parents to see when they pick up their child at the end of the day?**

- **Having an open door policy at the end of the day – how are you showing that you are open to a quick catch-up?**

- **When parents are invited into school, how accessible is the space?**

- **Language prompts – some schools I have worked in have had key policies and procedures translated into different languages.**

- **Have an agreed greeting for every parent. Be led by them on this and do your best to remember!**

- **Are your communications to parents as open and inclusive as they can be? Do you review them with a fresh pair of eyes to see if you are inadvertently offending or excluding anyone?**

- **Consider the timing of events so that as many parents as possible can be there. Offering a range of times means you can get more parents through the door.**

BUILDING RELATIONSHIPS BY ACTIVELY INVITING PARENTS TO SCHOOL

We spend our working lives in our school buildings and it can be easy to assume that parents understand exactly 'how things work'. Actively challenging these assumptions and inviting parents into school can have a huge impact on home–school relationships and can actively benefit both sides. If this exercise is conducted effectively, the parent will feel their perspective is truly valued and the school can use the experience to grow and develop.

FLIPPING THE FRAME: WATCH YOUR LANGUAGE

Our research and experience reveal a striking and concerning theme when it comes to the narrative around parents within schools: the language reveals a clear negativity bias. Mention 'parents' and teachers are likely to think of 'difficult', 'pushy' parents or 'hard-to-reach parents', with the barely concealed implication that these parents are making themselves deliberately elusive. Rather than saying 'working with' or 'collaborating with' parents, teachers tend to use 'dealing with', with implications of inconvenience and awkwardness.

A significant minority of parents in our survey wrote of 'gaslighting' by teachers, feeling 'ignored', 'dismissed' or 'blocked' by them. Some wrote with resignation of closed doors and teachers being 'too busy' to listen.

The emotional investment in children, and the associations with guilt, shame and feelings of judgement or inadequacy on both sides, makes this negativity understandable, but its impact is pernicious and it is essential that we, as educators, examine our language, question our biases and, above all, never assume.

HARD-TO-REACH PARENTS OR HARD-TO-REACH SCHOOLS?

In meetings up and down the country, there are fraught discussions over the conundrum of how to engage the minority of parents who appear unwilling to build relationships with the school. There are many factors which contribute to parental distrust, wariness or fear of school. The following three factors emerged most strikingly from our research:

1 **Parents' own experience of schools**. If parents' experience of school was difficult or traumatic, they will bring these memories and associated emotions into the school hall at parents' evenings. Building understanding and relationships is key.

2 **Class and hierarchies**. School staff, and particularly those in the most senior roles, will frequently be perceived as unapproachable because of some of our deeply ingrained social hierarchies and class systems. Humanising school staff is key!

3 **Unconscious bias**. Our society is fraught with inequity and discrimination. Even professionals carry their own sets of assumptions. We must seek to challenge these, whether it is the treatment of a certain ethnic group based on ignorance, or the arbitrary and unhelpful labelling of children and families.

If parents aren't engaging with school, the onus is on the school to change what it's doing rather than assign blame or resort to frustration. There could be any number of reasons for this and reaching out to discover what the factors are is the school's responsibility. Consider, for example, the factors outlined in the following Reflection. After each one, considering what is in your control and that of your school, make a note of what you might *do* to address them. You may wish to do this activity with your team.

 REFLECTION

The parents' own experience of school

Sitting outside the Head's office, or perching in a child's school chair, has the power to bring back a myriad of complex emotions for parents. In their book, *The Four Pillars of Parental Engagement*, Robbins and Dempster (2021: 41) reveal that 38% of parents are fearful of school, and this fear is often based on negative personal experiences.

What action could you take to overcome this?

The parents' own responsibilities outside school

The parent is working, or has caring responsibilities, during the hours when open events and parent consultations take place.

What action could you take to overcome this?

Information not getting to parents

Despite the information being on the website and emailed out, the parents have either not received it or not remembered it.

What action could you take to overcome this?

HUMANITY OVER PERFORMATIVITY

I make parents tremble in fear when I call home:
Hi. This is Mr. Mali. I hope I haven't called at a bad time,
I just wanted to talk to you about something your son said today.
To the biggest bully in the grade, he said,
'Leave the kid alone. I still cry sometimes, don't you?
It's no big deal.'
And that was the noblest act of courage I have ever seen.
I make parents see their children for who they are
and what they can be.

Taylor Mali, What Teachers Make (2022)

 HINTS AND TIPS

Start a parents' evening appointment not with a test score,
but with a comment on the child as a human being. You could
comment on their resilience, their sense of humour, their
helpfulness or their kindness.

Acknowledge the great work the parent is doing with the child
at home. If you think the parent should feel proud of their child,
tell them so, and tell them why! A mere post-it note sent home
to capture a magic moment is likely to have pride of place on the
fridge for years.

A NAMED PERSON

For parents, having a human point of contact at school can really help to
build the relationship. Rather than having 'school' flash up when their
telephone rings, it is so much better to be able to know that it's Wendy,
who knows their child really well and whom they trust.

BE PRESENT

Use transitions and routines to be as present as possible to parents at the school gate or on the playground. This gives parents structured but informal access to you and you to them.

COURAGE AND COMPASSION

Courage gives us a voice and compassion gives us an ear. Without both, there is no opportunity for empathy and connection.
Brené Brown (2007)

There is a time and a place for examining self-doubt and impostor syndrome but when working with parents, we need to put these to one side and remember that we are qualified experts in whom parents *must* have trust in order for children to thrive.

It is essential that, whether by email, in person or on the phone, we give these interactions our full attention; that we are brave and honest and take the time to show we care. Above all, we need to build boundaries around time and space in order to really, really listen.

NOTE IT DOWN!

TIME TO BUILD BRIDGES

THINK OF A PARENT WHOSE CHILD WOULD BENEFIT FROM AN IMPROVED RELATIONSHIP WITH SCHOOL. THIS COULD BE SOMEONE YOU HAVEN'T HAD CONTACT WITH FOR A WHILE OR SOMEONE WHOSE RELATIONSHIP WITH THE SCHOOL HAS FACED A SETBACK. PRIORITISE REBUILDING THAT RELATIONSHIP.

WHAT STEPS WILL YOU TAKE?

WHAT LANGUAGE WILL YOU USE?

GIVEN THE POWER OF LANGUAGE, IT CAN BE USEFUL TO SCRIPT WHAT YOU WANT TO SAY. IF IT IS A CHALLENGING CONVERSATION YOU NEED TO HAVE, YOU MAY WISH TO CONSULT CHAPTER 4.

CHAPTER 4
COMMUNICATION

This chapter explores the ideas that:

- Prioritising what matters most is essential
- Honesty and positivity are at the heart of effective communication
- Detailed preparation and accurate record-keeping are key to effective parental consultation meetings.

PRIORITIES AND ACCOUNTABILITY

> *The key to juggling is to know that some of the balls you have in the air are made of plastic and some are made of glass.*
> *Nora Roberts (Stephens, 2020)*

In a speech to new mothers, Nora Roberts referred to the act of juggling and of distinguishing between the glass and plastic balls. This metaphor can be equally applied to working in schools. We need to learn to distinguish between the glass and plastic balls; the biggest and most precious priorities and the things that seem to demand our attention but which actually won't matter five days, weeks or months from now.

'Busy-ness' is part of teachers' DNA. We are often juggling so many partners in this thing we call education: children (first and foremost), line managers, colleagues, external agencies and families. It is very hard to prioritise these, of course, and yet we feel achingly accountable to them all. Some days it can feel as if all the balls are made of glass! There is no science to ordering the priorities here. Parents will expect you to prioritise their children, but will also expect a proportion of your time. When that is an urgent request, it is easy for families to forget that you have lots of other things on too, and can't come to the phone at 11am on a Wednesday morning.

 HINTS AND TIPS

Prioritising what really matters

1   Spending time building relationships will mean that you are serving parents and families without needing to actively demonstrate it.

2   Manage expectations about time. Respond to a request quickly, if only to say that you have a full teaching day and a staff meeting after school, but that you will look into their concern and come back to them in a timely manner.

3   Work with your team. Is this an administrative request that can be managed by the superhero on the front desk? Do you need to bring the Senior Leadership Team (SLT) in to support you, who might also be out of class and able to deal with something more promptly than you?

4   Think about the means of communication. An email can be quick and easy for a short answer. A call may save you from email tennis late into the night. Think before you respond about what would be best for you in the long run.

5   Remember that you're not alone – you're one of a team working around the child and you all have a role to play.

HONESTY

We all know the old adage 'honesty is the best policy'. This is certainly the case in education – whether we are talking about how an Early Years pupil has found their first few days, or sharing a complicated situation at home. The more each side of the partnership knows about a child, the better care they can receive in a tailored manner. For honesty to thrive, there needs to be a bedrock of respect, and a shared vision that you are all there for the same reason: to secure the best outcome and experience for the child. We cannot just expect this relationship to materialise: we have to nurture it and make it grow, much in the same way we do in the relationships we have with our pupils.

Communication is key to growing an honest and open relationship. This stems from that first encounter, whether that is a brief introduction on the playground as you dismiss one child, referee an impromptu football game, send a pupil back for their coat (despite your third reminder) or at a more formal event, such as the September curriculum evening. Each encounter is a chance to build that relationship.

HINTS AND TIPS

Start each encounter with a smile and a positive comment.

1   Link your key messages to the values and vision of the school.

2   Talk openly about your desire to build positive and honest relationships with all parents.

3   Acknowledge that while there will be many positive inter-actions, there may be times when you need to collaborate on a sticky problem, and that the best way to do that is through open and supportive dialogue.

4   Remind everyone that you are all striving for the same thing: to get the best for and from the child at the heart of it all.

THE POWER OF POSITIVITY

We all know the impact of a negative comment – many studies have been conducted into the perfect positive:negative comment ratio! Gottman and Leveson (1999) pitch this at 3:1, although some go so far as to state it is 10:1. Whatever the exact ratio, the headlines are the same. You cannot always go in with the negative comment; you need to share the good news too. This is entirely relevant for parents too. The power of a positive phone call is huge. Try to end your week with a couple of these as part of your routine – it will make you feel good too!

DIFFICULT CONVERSATIONS

We can all pinpoint times when we have had to have a difficult conversation with a parent. Sometimes these will be about behaviour or academic progress. It may be about a change in circumstance. For many educators we have spoken to, the difficult conversations often stem from safeguarding issues and situations within the family. These are deeply complex conversations that you must never approach without the guidance and support of your safeguarding team.

 ## CASE STUDY

A child at school, whom we will call Jo, had been presenting 'out of sorts'. Their teacher noticed that while normally on time and well presented, Jo started to come in late and looking scruffy. They didn't have the right equipment in school and their lunch looked hastily pulled together. As is so often the case with these things, beyond the examples above, there was nothing concrete to go on, yet something just didn't feel right. The teacher rightly took this to their safeguarding lead, who asked them to continue to monitor Jo and share if anything else happened. While things didn't get worse, they also didn't get better. So the teacher decided to call Jo's parents. No one picked up, no one returned messages and no one responded to emails. Jo's teacher's concerns increased. Knowing Jo did sports club after school, Jo's teacher decided to pop out and watch for the last five minutes, where they could then catch whoever was collecting Jo for a quick catch up.

Luckily, Jo's mum was collecting and, just like Jo, she didn't seem like herself. When the teacher asked how she was, she became teary and would not make eye contact. Jo's teacher reassured her and suggested that she pop in for a cup of tea the next day, before drop-off. Through kindness and reassurance that they both wanted to make sure Jo was OK, they were able to get Jo's mum in. Over a cup of tea and a gentle conversation, Jo's mum was eventually able to disclose that things were not good at home and that Jo might have picked up on this. With support, the situation was shared and escalated to the Designated Safeguarding Lead (DSL), and Jo and the family are now getting the support that they need.

Had that gentle conversion not happened on the sideline, things may have been so different. But how do you begin those sensitive and so often difficult conversations? And who is best placed to have them?

Please note that the following section is looking at more generic tricky conversations, not deeply personal and complex ones which arise from sensitive areas.

When you need to have a difficult conversation, it will be made far easier by the fact you have already built that open and honest relationship with the parent or carer of the child in question using the tips above. Start by reminding the parent that you have the best interests of the child at heart.

 ## HINTS AND TIPS

How to have difficult conversations: NEFIART

Andy Buck (2018) has a great acronym for having a difficult conversation: NEFIART. This is usually in relation to leadership and working with others, but is just as relevant to communicating with parents.

If you follow it, it will help you to stay focused and calm and to cover every aspect of what you want to communicate. Some people find it useful to practise with a colleague in advance.

N name

E exemplify

F feelings

I importance

A accept

R resolve

T them

Taken from: https://andybuckblog.wordpress.com/2018/08/01/difficult-conversations/

The idea with NEFIART is that this can apply to any difficult conversation. I will give an example below:

N – I am just giving you a ring with regards to Charlie and their approach in the classroom at the moment. I am concerned they aren't showing their usual enthusiasm in class.

E – Let me give you an example. This morning, when I shared the title for our latest project, they were quick to roll their eyes and make a sarcastic comment to their partner.

F – I feel that we need to nip this in the bud now as I can see a habit forming and I know how much potential Charlie has in this subject.

I – It is really important that we are all coming from the same place so that Charlie knows we are all rooting for them.

A – I acknowledge that they might be thinking about other things, and that my subject is one small piece of the pie! However, it might be endemic of how Charlie is feeling about school in general.

R – Have you been aware of Charlie's feelings towards this subject recently?

T – Let's agree an approach moving forwards. Please do let Charlie know that we have had this conversation and I will then back this up again with them tomorrow.

SCHOOLS ARE DIFFERENT NOW

If we had a pound for every time a parent said to us, 'Gosh, it wasn't like this in my day', I would be significantly better off! One thing we nearly all have in common is that we attended a form of education for at least part of our lives. Everyone has a story to tell. Some of us are lucky enough for that to be largely positive, albeit with a few corkers we still dine out on. Others had a torrid time, leaving deep scars and a spectrum of emotions which remain at the core. We cannot ever rewrite that, but we can set a new tone for how adults perceive school. We can best address this through our manner with parents and the empathy we hold in every encounter.

On a practical level, we can also use our teaching skills to share with parents the new curriculum and the strategies that we teach the children, such as curriculum workshops looking at how we divide, modelled phonics sessions that demonstrate blending and decoding, or specialist sessions on e-safety. Knowledge is power and the more that parents know about how we teach now, the better equipped they will be to support their children.

SOCIAL MEDIA

Like it or loathe it, social media is here to stay and it makes up a big part of how our communities grow and communicate. Of course, there will be many school policies on this, which you must take note of and always adhere to. Social media such as Twitter and Instagram can be real sources of continuous professional development (CPD) and support, but it is very easy to link your social media use back to your school, so it is imperative to think about how each post might be perceived by a parent or boss.

Various schools use social media to promote their schools and to give parents almost live updates of what is happening in the classroom. This can be a great (and free) tool to showcase the brilliant things going on, but can also open up discussion and comment, so it is key that it is always being monitored.

WhatsApp can be a real scourge on teachers' time, with parents' groups sharing incorrect information. Fixing it can feel like a daunting, time-consuming and impossible task. To avoid this, speak to parents directly, get timely and accurate information out via the official school channels, and work with parents on a one-to-one basis so that they do not need to rely on WhatsApp to know what is going on. Ultimately, you cannot control what parents say and how they communicate, but you can ensure that the quality of your school communication is so good that they only use social media to peer into their child's world and to celebrate the good stuff!

 CASE STUDY

When he arrived at the school two years ago as the new Headteacher, one Headteacher found social media a real headache. Misinformation, misconceptions and whinging about the school were rife on Facebook. He has since made it his business to 'keep an eye' on all pages relating to the school. 'I have my ways', he says. Where issues arise, he addresses them directly in his weekly newsletter to parents, from the reasons why consistency around uniform is important, through to the fact that, no, Year 7 parents are not expected to print out the History booklet!

This Headteacher has combined a forensic attention to detail with an active effort to take control of the situation. He's letting the community know that he's watching and listening – even when they might not expect it! Most importantly, he's letting them know that he cares what they think and is responding to it.

 EXERCISE

Knowledge is power!

Task a key member (or group) of staff with getting out there and seeing what's being said by parents and families about your school and its staff on social media. This will require both time and a thick skin but is worth the effort. Key points to consider:

- Where positive and complimentary things are being said about the school and its staff, can these be captured and shared with staff or the wider community?

(Continued)

- Where there are negative ideas or questions being shared, what lies behind these comments? Does the issue require a rethink of a policy, an assembly with students, a talk with a particular student, or simply a reminder of a policy or procedure that might have been forgotten?

- Choose your battles. Which areas are worth picking up and addressing and which can be noted but shelved... for now? Some issues may balance themselves out in the discussions that follow – you may find other parents speaking out in defence of the school!

Many schools and Trusts now survey parents, and we know, of course, that the parent survey is part of Ofsted and Independent Schools' Inspectorate (ISI) inspection regimes. Forewarned is forearmed, so think about how the information garnered through such surveys can be used as a tool for good: to understand parental perception, to act on useful suggestions and to better understand the reality for a key stakeholder. Take the comments with a constructive mindset and it can be a very formative process.

PARENT CONSULTATIONS

Getting parent consultations right is a constant challenge for schools. In our experience, most teachers find that there is never enough time, there are parents who hover and need longer, and there are parents who often won't show up. The recent move to online consultations as a result of Covid lockdowns has worked like a dream for many, while others would prefer face-to-face contact. Some subject teachers find that their time with parents feels squeezed, whilst others feel their subject gets a much more intense focus. Whatever you personally think about parent consultations, they are part of how the vast majority of schools communicate with parents so we need to get good at them!

HINTS AND TIPS

Here are some helpful hints and tips for when it comes to those golden 10 minutes which never seem enough!

Fail to prepare – prepare to fail!

- The time flies and there is so much you want to get across. Write down headlines of what you can celebrate, in terms of attitude as well as progress. Also be clear on what you want to get from the meeting so that you can reach agreement.

- Have a clear target that you want the pupil to achieve – ideally, you will have shared this with the pupil prior to the meeting.

- Cut out the fluff! Time is of the essence and parents don't want a generic summary of what has been covered this term – they want to know about their child and what they need to do more of!

- Depending on school policy, consider taking examples of work and the child's book to evidence what you are talking about.

Record keeping is key!

- Take detailed notes of the conversation so that both parties are clear on discussion points if they are then revisited later in the year.

- Note down any action for yourself and build time into your next Planning, Preparation and Assessment (PPA) time to do what you said you would do.

(Continued)

- If possible, give parents time to ask questions. However, if they are leading to a bigger conversation, feel free to suggest a follow-up meeting or a call rather than rush something that the parent considers is important.

Above all else, work with the ethos of the law of no surprises. If you need to have a trickier conversation, parent consultation meetings should not be the first time the parent is hearing about it.

End on a positive. By that, we don't mean make up some vacuous compliment that has not been earned! If there is something positive to share, which there nearly always is, then use that. Otherwise, your positive sign off can be the fact that you are both keen to work towards the same goal, or that you have agreed a target that is achievable.

NOTE IT DOWN!

Go right back to basics on communication with parents in the context of your role.

What are the three most important things you want parents to know/understand about how you work with their child?

How are these communicated?

How do you know that all parents know what they need to know and how can you remind them without swamping them?

How can communication in these three key areas be more effective?

CHAPTER 5
GETTING THE BALANCE RIGHT

This chapter explores the ideas that:

- Binary thinking is unhelpful and can be actively damaging
- Teachers *and* parents need boundaries
- Careful sharing of key information is powerful.

BEWARE BINARY THINKING

Human beings have a strong dramatic instinct toward binary thinking, a basic urge to divide things into two distinct groups, with nothing but an empty gap in between. We love to dichotomize. Good versus bad. Heroes versus villains. My country versus the rest. Dividing the world into two distinct sides is simple and intuitive, and also dramatic because it implies conflict, and we do it without thinking, all the time.
Hans Rosling (2019)

Working with the hopes, fears and expectations of other human beings is a messy business and in order to be as effective as we can at engaging parents with school, we have little choice but to embrace the messiness. When teachers and parents consider one another, particularly when they feel stressed by the weight of perceived expectations, the language quickly moves into frustrated generalisation, as discussed in Chapter 3.

The truth is that no parent becomes a parent without wanting the best for their child and no teacher steps into the profession without genuinely wanting to do a good job. The barriers to both of these aims are countless and the societal measure of what makes a 'good' parent and a 'good' teacher are frequently judgemental and unhelpful.

MORE BINARY THINKING TO CHALLENGE IN SCHOOLS

THEM AND US

These are terms often heard in schools to describe various groups (children and adults, teaching staff and SLT, parents and teachers) and can be equally unhelpful. As described in Chapter 1, focusing on what unites us is key.

NEGATIVE AND POSITIVE CONTACT WITH HOME

It is of course our duty to inform parents when children are struggling with their learning or conduct, but we can all too easily find ourselves making contact with home for negative reasons far more than for positive ones. Do yourselves – and your parents – a favour and make a conscious decision to even the balance: for every difficult or negative call you have to make, make another to congratulate or praise a child!

CHALLENGING THE DEFICIT MODEL

As educators, we can be quick to make assumptions about the families we work with. Have a look at the case study below (which has been anonymised, but is based on many true stories!) and then consider the questions in the Reflection that follows.

 CASE STUDY

Kay, a parent of a child in Year 5, is the subject of regular discussions in the school. Her son's academic progress is behind where the data suggests it should be. He frequently arrives at school looking dishevelled and with a packet of crisps which he says is 'breakfast'. Kay rarely answers her phone when the school tries to contact her and rarely attends parent consultation meetings. On the rare occasions when she has attended meetings in school, staff have reported that she appears defensive and is sometimes rude.

 REFLECTION

It is easy to assume that Kay is being deliberately difficult, but take a moment to consider what might be going on beneath the surface. What steps would you take to engage with Kay? What might be going on for Kay? You may wish to consider the following:

(Continued)

- **The impact of Covid-19 and the cost-of-living crisis on families, their mental health, their working arrangements, their routines, and so on.**

- **Kay's own experience of school.**

- **Why Kay might be unwilling to engage – what are her working hours? Does she feel judged? Has a safe space been created for her to speak and really be heard?**

THE IMPACT OF COVID-19

As discussed in Chapter 1, during the pandemic, schools stepped willingly into the breach where other services were forced to close or operate from home. Contrary to unhelpful headlines, almost all primary, SEND and Early Years settings remained open to those who needed them most. Many schools report that levels of need in terms of safeguarding, vulnerability, mental health and SEND rose sharply – and continue to do so.

Of course, Covid-19 isn't over and this is another unhelpful binary narrative: neither can we ignore the pandemic nor can we allow it to dominate our thinking. Curriculum and standards must of course remain priorities too. Covid-19 isn't an 'excuse' for underachievement. This narrative is equally unhelpful, but to ignore the fact that the 'gaps' in our society have become chasms is not an option.

There was another theme which arose from the beginning of the pandemic regarding the opportunities for fresh thinking that came with Covid-19. These opportunities brought into stark relief the importance of relationships, the role of schools as a safe and non-judgemental source of structure and reliability for parents and children, and the rapid increase in competence with online communication. One governor refers to 'Covid keeps' – the things we learned to value more highly and the approaches we learned to take which had real value.

 REFLECTION

What are your 'Covid keeps' as an educator? What old and less positive habits will you avoid going back to?

BALANCE AND BOUNDARIES

Teaching is a never-ending story. The work is never over; the job is never done.
Andy Hargreaves (1994)

Many parents in our survey are sympathetic to the demands on teachers, as one parent commented: 'Teaching staff have great workloads and often it can be difficult to have time for the communication needed.' The desire for more dedicated time for face-to-face communication is expressed frequently. In some cases, the apparent lack of time for them and their child can leave parents feeling misunderstood and undervalued.

It's a truism that teachers can't do their jobs effectively if they are frazzled and worn out, so while putting boundaries in place and clarifying expectations might feel like 'just another job' to do, it's in everyone's interests to spend the time doing so.

 EXERCISE

Adapt the table below (timings have deliberately been left blank so you can adapt it to your own schedule) to show when you *can* be available to parents. Grab yourself some highlighters or coloured pens in green, 'amber' and red. Depending on your role, 3–4 sessions a week is usually more than enough! Green represents total availability, so block out this time to focus on parents. If no one gets in touch with you, use it to reach out to them. Amber represents the times when you are willing to check emails or your work phone for important issues. Red represents the times when you are not available. At these times you should signpost to parents who else can be available to them in school.

You may wish to add 'codes' to show what kinds of communication you will focus on at given times.

☺ **Available for face-to-face communication**

📞 **Available for telephone communication**

✉ **Available for online communication**

Some teachers have indicated that it is helpful for parents to understand what they are doing with the rest of their time, so by all means indicate this too – teaching, PPA, meetings, days and times when you don't work.

	Monday	Tuesday	Wednesday	Thursday	Friday
Session 1 (__:__ – __:__)					
Session 2 (__:__ – __:__)					
Session 3 (__:__ – __:__)					
Session 4 (__:__ – __:__)					
Session 5 (__:__ – __:__)					
Session 6 (__:__ – __:__)					
Optional evening session*					

* We would suggest a maximum of one evening session per week per staff member

Depending on your role and situation, you may wish to incorporate a weekly or fortnightly 'surgery' when your door is open to parents who wish to speak to you (and whose own commitments allow them to).

Remember! Handled effectively, you are likely to gain as much from these conversations as you are required to give.

PARENTS NEED BALANCE AND BOUNDARIES TOO!

Why not ask the parents of your students to do the same in your communications with them early in the year? If they can let you know when they're most likely to be available, this will really help to streamline communications. This could also be a good opportunity to clarify the names they would like you to use and the best medium of communication.

SHARING INTELLIGENCE

There was a time in schools when sensitive information about families was shared regularly with the entire school community. Fortunately, things have changed and there is now an emphasis on respecting the privacy of our parents and children as much as we would that of our colleagues. Designated Safeguarding Leads, SENDCos and pastoral leads will often, quite rightly, hold such sensitive information and will only share with teachers what they need to know. But there is soft data that can be collected through contact with parents that can really help us support students effectively in the classroom.

 HINTS AND TIPS

Soft data has power. In your search to build fruitful relationships with parents, you may wish to use opportunities (on the gate, at parents' evening, etc.) to find out a bit more about the following:

- **Parents' hopes and aspirations for their children**

- **How much time/capacity parents have to support their children with learning at home**

- Parents' skills, experiences and strengths (and whether they'd be happy/willing to share them at school)

- Parents' anxieties and fears with a view to signposting them to where support can be found.

BALANCE AND EMOTIONAL RESPONSES

We have established that our work requires a profound investment of self, so when parents feel they or their children have been ignored or let down, reactions can be emotional. Likewise, teachers take pride in their work and feeling that a parent isn't working collaboratively with them can be deeply frustrating and even upsetting. While the emotional investment can be a positive thing – it shows how much we care – it's important to step back and gain perspective. In the words of one teacher in our survey:

> [Recognise] that when a parent is angry, they aren't angry with you personally. You're just the nearest thing to an authority figure they have to take their frustrations out on. It's far better to let them vent and listen quietly, rather than jump straight in.

SUPPORTING PARENTS THROUGH CHANGE

There's a widespread understanding from both parents and teachers that the relationships change dramatically as children get older. In Early Years settings, a parent can expect to get regular updates on toileting and mealtimes as well as development and progress, whereas by the time they get to secondary school, the onus is more frequently on the child to convey key information and take responsibility for their own learning.

Transitions – from one phase of schooling to the next or from one school to another – constitute critical incidents in families' lives and have to be managed carefully by schools. Again, the impact of Covid-19 on what is in many schools already a carefully choreographed process cannot be underestimated (ask any Early Years teacher about the first 100 days and what our three and four year olds have potentially missed).

Here are a few top tips on managing transitions:

- Be patient with ourselves, our parents and our children – we're doing our best to manage the factors within our control.

- Capitalise on how technology has developed: use images and video footage to prepare students for change.

- It's not just about lessons! Include toilets, corridors, eating spaces and changing rooms, timings and routines.

- Create links between children already in the school and those preparing to move to it – a chance to exchange letters, emails and anecdotes can take the fear out of change.

One way to help parents is to prepare them for the transition. Here are some useful ways that you can do that:

- Call parents in or meet them online to share what they can expect from the transition and what they can do to help their child to transition. For instance, as they come into Reception, they can help to make sure their children are toilet trained and can hold their cutlery. They can help them to get quicker at buttons and putting their shoes on the right feet! You can even invite an external speaker to support this, such as a parenting expert or a child development expert, who can add ideas and share the thinking behind your approach.

- As they move from Key Stage to Key Stage, keep inviting parents in. Keep telling them what is expected this time around! How are you as a school developing independence, and how can parents support that? Also be crystal clear about what parents can expect from the school. Primary parents are used to seeing teachers at pick up and drop-off but is that the same at secondary school? A forgotten PE kit can be called for and dropped off at primary school, but will that continue at secondary school? How does the behaviour system change?

NOTE IT DOWN!

WITH THAT IN MIND, JOT DOWN WHAT YOU WISH YOUR PARENTS KNEW BEFORE THEIR CHILDREN GOT TO YOUR CLASS OR KEY STAGE.

- WHAT I WISH THEY KNEW

- WHAT I WISH THEIR CHILDREN COULD DO

- HOW PARENTS MIGHT BE ABLE TO SUPPORT THAT

- HOW I MIGHT COMMUNICATE THAT

TAKE EVERY 'GOSH, I WISH THEY COULD JUST _____ THEMSELVES' AND SHARE THAT BEFORE THE CHILD GETS TO YOU!

CHAPTER 6
EFFICIENCY AND EFFECTIVENESS

This chapter explores the ideas that:

- Parents and teachers must develop a shared ethos
- Parenting styles have a profound impact on children and a growth mindset is worth nurturing
- Start with why: be clear, precise and proactive in your communication.

One of our favourite questions is always, so what? Not in a dismissive way, but really questioning the impact of what we have read, or heard, or seen. You have committed time to read our research and our musings. This final section is for you to crystallise those 'take aways' and make sure your commitment was a sound investment of your time – time that we all know is so precious!

As Steven Covey reminded us all on Twitter (ironically, the place where I lose a great deal of time!):

> *The key is in not spending time, but in investing it.*
> Stephen R. Covey (Covey et al. 1995)

Hopefully you have had the chance to reflect and to think about your own relationships with parents. But to what end?

 # REFLECTION

Take five minutes now to jot down the following:

Key reflections

What am I going to do as a result of reading this book?

Keep your pencil in your hand, as we hope this final chapter will give you more things to add as you go!

TEACHERS AND PARENTS: CHICKEN AND EGG

When we sat down to plan this book, we ummed and ahhed for some time, thinking about all the different areas we could visit as part of this little guide. In the end, we focused on the main reader being the educator. You could write a whole tome about parenting – indeed, many have – but we decided to focus on our target team: those of you who work with children and parents on a daily basis. That said, we hope we have made it clear how integral that relationship is, and so it would be remiss of us to not consider parents in more detail.

PARENTS AND TEACHERS: THE IMPORTANCE OF A SHARED APPROACH

If we take the average week at school as being about 32.5 hours for children, then we really don't have them for very long at all! There are 168 hours in a week. That is 32.5 with us at school and 135.5 at home, meaning that parents have them over 80% of the time, and us just under 20% of the time! Then take into account holidays and half terms! This means it is so important that parents and schools share an approach: a shared ethos for what we are seeking to do and how we are seeking to do it.

Take, for example, the issue of mindset. Many of you will be well versed in the work of Dr Carol Dweck (2017) and Matthew Syed (2018), who both examine the concept of growth mindset. Many schools have adopted this approach, seeking to develop in their pupils an open mindset, the ability to make and learn from mistakes, and to see failure as a central facet of learning. This, however, can surely only be successfully embedded if parents also adopt the approach.

 REFLECTION

Think about your own mindset. When I ask you to think of a time when you failed, how does that make you feel? What has led you to feeling that way?

As a teacher, I bet you encourage mistake making and failure on a daily basis. But do you embrace it in quite the same way?

Clemmie doesn't mind admitting an abject fear of failure and can trace this back to being in an academically ambitious school where results were everything. Pupils were ranked and ordered by how well they performed in tests, how many times they represented the school and, ultimately, by the 13+ outcomes. Following in the footsteps of a highly gifted brother didn't help!

What does your story look like, and how does that impact on you now?

PARENTING STYLES

Clemmie did a great deal of research into parenting styles when presenting a TEDx talk entitled 'Does snowplough parenting remove grit?' (Stewart and Glover, 2020). In this talk, she and her colleague explored various types of parenting and the impact those styles had on the children in their care, and on children across a variety of schools within their Multi Academy Trust. From 'helicopter parents', who hover over their children all the time, to 'snowplough parents', who forge ahead of their child, removing any barrier to success and happiness, parents can't help but seek to protect their children. But are they unwittingly failing their children by preventing them from experiencing failure and emotion? Clemmie's favourite term was the 'curling parent', who smoothes out any friction so that the child has a seamless path through life.

 REFLECTION

Think about your own parents. What approach did they take with you? Were they 'free range', letting you just get on with it? Were they 'tiger parents', wading in and fighting on your behalf whenever you were seemingly wronged? How has this impacted on you, as an adult, as a teacher, and perhaps even as a parent?

The crux of Clemmie and Rebecca's TEDx talk was to advocate a new approach – one which they think they have coined – and that is the 'trampoline parent'. These parents allow their children to bounce up and experience independent flight for themselves, but they remain there to wrap around them when they fall, before letting them bounce back up to try it all over again. The hope is that each time they bounce a little higher, experience more independence and gain the skills that will prepare them to fly on their own as they grow up.

If the school and the parent have a completely different ethos, the child will constantly be in a state of flux, meeting the needs of one, while disappointing the other!

 ## CASE STUDY

Georgie returns home from school to share that her recent spelling test yielded a 6/10, much to the disappointment of her pushy parents. They expect to see 10/10 each week, providing clear evidence that their child is gifted and is working hard. Georgie, on the other hand, is delighted with her 6, safe in the knowledge that her teacher is pleased with the progress she made from 5/10 last week. There are two competing influences in her life: two competing approaches, with entirely different pressures. Who wins? Certainly not Georgie!

Here is another example from Clemmie's days as a Year 5 teacher. Back when endless homework projects were a thing, she set the task for children to research, design and build an Anderson shelter that could withstand water damage and colliding with a cricket ball. Over the weeks, projects were dragged into her classroom, made with varying levels of effort, expertise and success. One, however, was delivered by a very proud-looking father, who placed it down, looked at her and asked her for her initial thoughts, while his son looked mortified behind him. It later became apparent that his father had completed the entire project, which was brought to Clemmie's notice by the father asking for personalised feedback. Short of also asking for house points, it was clear the project was his baby. Perhaps he just had a passion for model making? More likely, he wanted his son's project to be the best. The father's approach prevented his son from failing, from learning or from getting anything whatsoever from the project.

I am sure we could all reel off a hundred examples of this sort of thing, where parents' involvement has been too great, too little, too fierce or too relaxed. So how do we go about improving the situation?

1   Start with why

To quote the great Simon Sinek (2011), starting with why is always a great place to begin. Why are we here? Why do we educate children? What do we want them to get from their time in our school? With clarity on these questions, we can then present our mission, vision and values in a clear and succinct way, so that parents can decide whether those align with their own.

2   Embed that as a member of the community

While point 1 will likely have been established by the SLT and trustees before you join a school, as a practitioner within the community, you need to embrace those values and feel that you can live and promote them every day. Part of that comes from your initial visit, and from the recruitment process. Ask questions, stress-test how that lives out day to day and think about how you can contribute to that. If your values and ethos clash, you will constantly struggle to make sure they align, and ensure they are the reason you bring your best self to work each day!

3   Think about how you can communicate those values clearly

Much of this sits with leadership, in terms of marketing material and website content, the school website and so on. But whatever level you currently work at within your school, how do you convey the ethos and mission of the school? Let's take an example. If a school states its desire to inspire curiosity and independence in the pupils, who are expected to show the values of respect, empathy and ambition, how does that appear in your sphere. On the walls? In the language of your dialogue? In your feedback? In your planning? In your team meetings? How about through your communication with parents? How could you enhance that further?

4   Be precise

Take every opportunity to drive those values home! When you call a parent, frame your feedback on those values. Reiterate the vocabulary at every given opportunity. If you are celebrating a child to a parent, what aspect of that chosen mindset did they show, and how? Target your celebration with precise words and real examples. Likewise, if a child has made a mistake, describe it in terms of the culture and values of the school, as well as providing a way to make amends. By reiterating the language and culture of the school in every interaction, you will be cementing your approach, your school's approach, and how parents can sit alongside that with a shared vision.

5   Communication is key!

One of the best pieces of advice I ever received was that whenever you write an email, imagine copying in the Head and the CEO. Most of the time, that made no difference to the style of my communication. Occasionally, I would adjust the tone slightly, or make it briefer, or indeed add more information! Each communication is a window to the parent about you and your values, so make sure it shows the best of you! If you are at the end of your tether, and something has really pushed you over the edge, then do not respond! Or send a polite holding email while you gather yourself. Occasionally, I would keyboard bash my response, send it to myself and by the next morning, I was ready to filter it down and rewrite it. I was always so glad I did! I would often ask my Deputy Head to read my response too, to sense check it and see how it would land with a fresh pair of eyes. At times, our passion can alter how we approach something, but ultimately, we are professionals, and we always need to respond as such, no matter how much patience it takes! Final tip – keep EVERY email and retain notes from every call or meeting. You never know when you might need to refer to them.

6   Be proactive

Think about how else you can take parents with you. Perhaps you can run an online training session that advocates the same approach you are using in school or share some literature that includes highlights of the research you use as the base of your approach in school. You can set a task where children explain a concept like growth mindset to their parents. You can arrange regular opportunities to get parents in to help shape the culture of the school, and its vision moving forwards, so that it belongs to the whole community and not just the staff. As a Head, I met with the Parents' Association every half term, to take their feedback, hear what they had to say and explain my decision making. I always used this time to reiterate our approaches and how they shaped aspects like homework, spelling (an ongoing bone of contention for many schools), sport for all, diversity and inclusion, trips and visits and so on. I framed every answer with an explicit link to our vision and values. This led to many great discussions and a real sense of partnership. We also took parents' ideas into consideration and many projects grew from this, the most successful one being a 'return to work' programme for parents which became a real network of support and encouragement, again reiterating our values as a community.

7   Embrace technology!

We could write a whole book on the gains made in the use of technology in education in the last two years during the Covid-19 pandemic. Luckily lots of other people are doing that! However, how can we use those gains to better support the relationship between home and school. Early Years parents love having access to apps to see observations and progress. Why not use apps that do a similar thing further up the school? Many parents struggle to get to parents' evening in person, not least because they have children to look after. So why not keep offering online consultations as an option? Why not continue to livestream big school events so that more of the family can tune in to see a child being celebrated or taking part in a performance? Many schools successfully use social media to open a window to school life, thus reiterating how things are done and how children's experiences are embraced.

FINALLY, KEEP IT SIMPLE!

> *Simple can be harder than complex. You have to work hard to get your thinking clean to make it simple. But it's worth it in the end because once you get there, you can move mountains. Move mountains in such a way that there will be no mountains to move.*
> *Steve Jobs (Reinhardt, 1998)*

Working effectively with parents is, as we've established, hugely complex, but we'd also argue that it's fundamentally very simple. Sweat the small stuff and pay attention to what, to you, might be tiny details but may matter hugely to parents. Be prepared to reflect and evolve as this glorious and terrifying world changes around us. Keep parents, alongside their children, front and centre of all decisions you make. Hold your values front and centre and remember that perfection is impossible when organic beings work with other organic beings. Remember that parenting and teaching are big, tough jobs, but are ultimately joyful ones and are definitely the most important ones there are. And remember that together, we can move mountains.

NOTE IT DOWN!

This final activity can be used to work through a specific issue or a bigger school policy, or when working with a single parent or carer. Answer the following questions, on your own or with your colleagues:

1   What are our core values when it comes to working with parents?

2   What do we believe we can achieve?

3   What resources/time/people/skills do we need?

4   What's our next best step? What then? And what then? (Be specific)

5   How will it look and feel when we've achieved our goal? What will children/parents/staff be saying?

REFERENCES

Arends, H. (Producer) (2003) *Disney Sing-Along Songs: Sing a Song with Pooh Bear and Piglet Too* [DVD]. Burbank, CA: Walt Disney Video.

Bronfenbrenner, U. (1979) *The Ecology of Human Development: Experiments by Nature and Design*. Cambridge, MA: Harvard University Press.

Brown, B. (2007) *I Thought It Was Just Me (But It Isn't)*. New York: Avery.

Buck, A. (2018) Difficult conversations. *Buck's Fizz* [Blog], 1 August. Available at: https://andybuckblog.wordpress.com/2018/08/01/difficult-conversations/ (Accessed: 9 August 2022).

Coalition for Youth Mental Health in Schools (2021) *Fixing a Failing System: Rethinking Mental Health Support in Schools for the Post-Covid Generation*. Nottingham: The Coalition for Youth Mental Health in Schools. Available at: www.publicfirst.co.uk/wp-content/uploads/2021/10/MHC-Report.pdf (Accessed: 9 August 2022)

Covey, S.R., Merrill, A.R. and Merrill, R.R. (1995) *First Things First*. New York: Simon and Schuster.

Department for Education (2022) *SEND and AP Green Paper: Responding to the Consultation*. Available at: https://www.gov.uk/government/publications/send-and-ap-green-paper-responding-to-the-consultation (Accessed: 9 August 2022)

Department for Education and Department of Social Care (UK Government) (2014) *SEND Code of Practice: 0 to 25 Years*. London: HM Government. Available at: www.gov.uk/government/publications/send-code-of-practice-0-to-25 (Accessed: 9 August 2022)

Dweck, C. (2017) *Mindset: Changing the Way You Think to Fulfil Your Potential* (Updated Edition). London: Robinson.

Evans, R. (1971) Richard Evans' Quote Book. Salt Lake City, UT: Publisher's Press.

Gottman, J. M. and Levenson, R. W. (1999) What predicts change in marital interaction over time? A study of alternative models. *Family Process*, *38*(2), 143–158. Available at: https://doi.org/10.1111/j.1545-5300.1999.00143.x (Accessed: 9 August 2022)

Hargreaves, A. (1994) *Changing Teachers, Changing Times: Teachers' Work and Culture in the Postmodern Age.* London: Cassell.

Harris, A. and Goodall, J. (2007) *Engaging Parents in Raising Achievement: Do Parents Know They Matter? A Research Project Commissioned by the Specialist Schools and Academies Trust.* London: Department for Children, Schools and Families. Available at: https://dera.ioe.ac.uk/6639/1/DCSF-RW004.pdf (Accessed: 9 August 2022)

Kallivayalil, R. A. and Thomas, S. P. (2019) Education begins at home. *Pallikkutam: A Complete Educational Portal* [Blog], 2 May. Available at: www.pallikkutam.com/blog/education-begins-at-home- (Accessed: 9 August 2022)

Kara, B. (2020) *A Little Guide for Teachers: Diversity in Schools.* London: Corwin UK.

Mali, T. (2022) What Teachers Make. Available at: https://taylormali.com/poems/what-teachers-make/ (Accessed: 19 August 2022).

Morgan, Z. (2019) Male teaching assistant 'sterotyped' as 'woman's job'. *BBC News*, 30 June. Available at: https://www.bbc.co.uk/news/uk-wales-48799505 (Accessed: 19 August 2022)

Ofsted (2021) *Inspecting Teaching of the Protected Characteristics in Schools.* London: Ofsted. Available at: www.gov.uk/government/publications/

inspecting-teaching-of-the-protected-characteristics-in-schools/inspecting-teaching-of-the-protected-characteristics-in-schools (Accessed: 9 August 2022).

Phillips, C. (2016) Around town: Sophie Grégoire-Trudeau leaves 'em feeling warm and fuzzy at Debra Dynes Family House event. *Ottawa Citizen*, 7 April. Available at: https://ottawacitizen.com/life/style/our-ottawa/around-town-sophie-gregoire-trudeau-leaves-em-feeling-warm-and-fuzzy-at-debra-dynes-family-house-event (Accessed: 9 August 2022).

Reinhardt, A. (1998) Steve Jobs: There's sanity returning, *BusinessWeek*, 25 May. Available at: https://www.bloomberg.com/news/articles/1998-05-25/steve-jobs-theres-sanity-returning (Accessed: 9 August 2022).

Robbins, J. and Dempster, K. (2021) *The Four Pillars of Parental Engagement: Empowering Schools to Connect Better with Parents and Pupils*. Camarthen: Independent Thinking Press.

Rosling, H. (2019) *Factfulness: Ten Reasons We're Wrong about the World – and Why Things Are Better Than You Think*. London: Hodder & Stoughton.

Siebel Newsom, J. (Director) (2011) *Miss Representation* [Film]. Girls' Club Entertainment.

Sinek, S. (2011) *Start with Why: How Great Leaders Inspire Everyone to Take Action*. London: Penguin.

Stephens, J. (2020) You're juggling glass balls and plastic balls. What you choose to drop changes everything. *Mammamia*, 9 October. Available at: https://www.mamamia.com.au/nora-roberts-glass-ball/ (Accessed: 9 August 2022).

Stewart, C. and Glover, R. (2020) Does snowplough parenting remove grit? June. Available at: https://www.ted.com/talks/rebecca_glover_clemmie_stewart_does_snowplough_parenting_remove_grit (Accessed: 9 August 2022)

Syed, M. (2018) *You are Awesome: Find Your Confidence and Dare to be Brilliant at (Almost) Anything*. London: Wren & Rook.

Taylor, S. (2015) *Use of Role and Power in Parent–Teacher Relationships: Perceptions from the Parent Perspective*. Dissertations and Theses, Paper 2324, Portland State University. Available at: https://doi.org/10.15760/etd.2321 (Accessed: 9 August 2022)

Tierney, S. (2020) *Educating with Purpose: The Heart of What Matters*. Woodbridge: John Catt.

UCL (2020) *Covid-19 Social Study*. London: University College London. Available at: www.covidsocialstudy.org/ (Accessed: 9 August 2022)

FURTHER READING

Evangelou, M., Coxon, K., Sylva, K., Smith, S. and Chan, L. S. (2013) Seeking to engage 'hard-to-reach' families: towards a transferable model of intervention. *Children & Society*, *27*(2), 127–138. https://doi.org/10.1111/j.1099-0860.2011.00387.x

Goodall, J. (2019) Top 10 tips for getting parents more involved in school life. *TES Magazine*, 9 April. Available at: www.tes.com/news/parental-engagement-top-10-tips-getting-parents-more-involved-school-life (Accessed: 9 August 2022)

Hannaghan, K. (2022) Purposeful parental engagement. In K. Evans, T. Hoyle, F. Roberts and B. Yusuf (eds), *The Big Book of Whole School Wellbeing* (pp. 131–138). London: SAGE.

Jafarov, J. (2015) Factors affecting parental involvement in education: the analysis of literature. *Journal of Humanities and Social Sciences*, 1 December. Available at: https://doi.org/10.5782/2223-2621.2015.18.4.35 (Accessed: 16 September 2022).

López, R. (2012) *Transforming Schools through Parent Engagement* [Podcast], Episode 110, Classnotes Podcast 110, 16 July. Available at: www.idra.org/resource-center/transforming-schools-through-parent-engagement/ (Accessed: 9 August 2022)

McCrea, E. (2021) *Brighter Thinking Pod – Episode 13: Engaging Parents in Education (Part 1)* [Podcast], 2 July. Available at: www.cambridge.org/us/education/blog/2021/07/02/brighter-thinking-pod-ep-13-engaging-parents/ (Accessed: 9 August 2022)

McCrea, E. (2021) *Brighter Thinking Pod – Episode 14: Engaging Parents in Education (Part 2)* [Podcast], 2 July. Available at: https://www.cambridge.org/us/education/blog/2021/07/02/brighter-thinking-pod-ep-14-engaging-parents-in-education-part-2/ (Accessed: 16 September 2022).

Parentkind: https://www.parentkind.org.uk/

Simmons, H. (2020) Feeling judged: parenting culture and interpersonal surveillance. In H. Simmons, *Surveillance of Modern Motherhood: Experiences of Universal Parenting Courses* (pp. 93–118). Basingstoke: Palgrave Macmillan.

INDEX